L for the lavender over the bed
M for the man that I love
N for the nasty bits stuck in the sink
O for the wings of a dove

A Book of
Bestial
Nonsense

from Simon Drew

A Book of
Bestial Nonsense
by Simon Drew

woken from a distant dream
with a sudden jerk
sitting in an onion patch
garden spirits lurk
humming tunes to soothe you, with
music while you work.

ANTIQUE COLLECTORS' CLUB,

I think I could turn and live with animals,
they are so placid and self-contain'd,
I stand and look at them long and long.
They do not sweat and whine about
their condition,
They do not lie awake in the dark and
weep for their sins,
They do not make me sick discussing
their duty to God,
Not one is dissatisfied, not one is demented
with the mania of owning things,
Not one kneels to another, nor to his
kind that lived thousands of years ago,
Not one is respectable or unhappy over
the whole earth.

Walt Whitman

ONE GOOD TERN DESERVES ANOTHER

© Simon Drew 1986
World copyright reserved
Reprinted October 1986
Reprinted November 1986
ISBN 1 85149 041 8

British Library data
Drew, Simon
  A book of bestial nonsense.
  I. Title   II. Antique Collectors' Club
  821'.914   PR6054.R4/

Published and printed in England by the Antique Collectors' Club Ltd.
Woodbridge, Suffolk

to
Caroline,
Plug
and the Dartmouth Vintners

In the beginning, at the start,
at the outset, in the van,
forefront, debut, hors d'oeuvre, dawn,
so the enterprise began:
herrings galloped, horses swam,
tigers flew and eagles ran.

INTODUCTION

The contents of this book are the
result of playing with words and
images.
 Writing rhymes is part of the
same mental process as doing
crosswords, solving anagrams and
singing nonsensical ditties - habits
instilled in childhood. Most people
are aware of the ambiguity of
certain words and phrases but
resist the temptation to play games
with them.
 The drawings are a celebration
of everyday objects and ordinary
events. There's a lot to be said
for the quick unposed holiday snap
that cuts off the feet or even, on
really exciting occasions, most of

people's heads. The "perfect" photo with three aunts in the centre (and no lamp-post coming out of the top of anyone's head) is not only very unrepresentative and unnatural but also extremely rare. It's better to draw things as they really are or could be even if this results in a picture that seems bizarre.

All nature can be revealed by one fragment: it's only necessary to represent accurately one simple thing to reflect the whole world.

And there's no need to be serious to express one's enjoyment of life.

a slug in a salad is rather a fright;
a fly in your tea is a miserable sight;
but one of the things that I utterly hate
is finding a hare on the side of my plate.

PUFFIN

the wily gannet sits on granite
thus avoiding germs
and so this bird must feed on fish
for granite has no worms.

the moon was wrapped in mist
like the clingfilm round a pear
and the hills were growing darker
and the milkman wasn't there.

At ten past four on Tuesday night
I saw a bull: the bull was dressed
in silken frock of pink and white
and underneath a woollen vest.

The beast had made the clothes itself,
the wool from sheep across the sea.
"I spun the silk" he said to me,
while gently sipping milky tea.

But since that day, I've now been told,
he's lost his cash and times are hard;
he has no clothes; they've all been sold
and now he's tied up in the yard.

No frock, no silk,
no vest, no wool,
no tea, no milk;
how now brown bull?

15

1 duck thinking—he's ignored; 2 ducks sleeping; 1 duck bored.

17

Stage one of this magic work
is choosing perfect fruit.
A healthy vine is what you need
from tip of leaf to toe of root.

Perfect Wine Making.....

Grapes are thrown in wooden baths
to pulp the liquid out:
the future wine will filter through
and trickle from the golden spout.

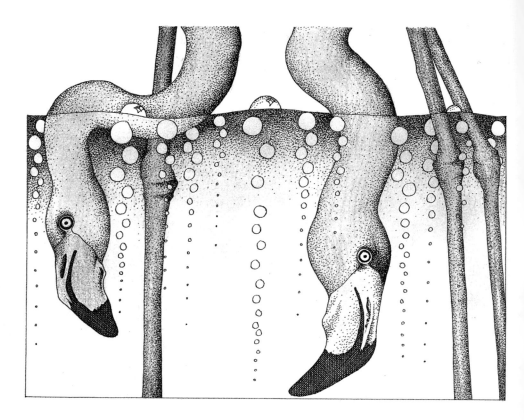

Then inspectors check the juice;
the fermentation starts.
Soon we have vin ordinaire
to clear our heads and warm our hearts.

When the bottles have been filled
the sampling must be done
(and never tire of doing this
until you've tasted every one).

if you sleep under blankets patterned with stripes
with your nose sticking out from the pillow
a passing zoologist might say you are
a five-banded (dead) armadillo.

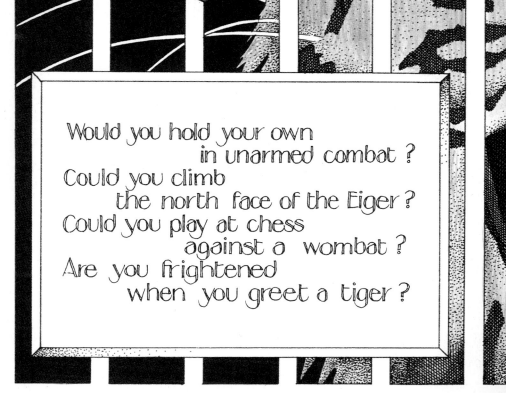

Would you hold your own
                 in unarmed combat ?
Could you climb
       the north face of the Eiger ?
Could you play at chess
            against a wombat ?
Are you frightened
      when you greet a tiger ?

The Breakfast Kit

Do you remember our breakfast
with cockles and kedgeree pie
and sausages shaped like bananas
and kidneys on toast? Nor do I.

Do I remember our breakfast:
the porridge that tasted of glue,
the bird sat alone on the terrace
and sang us a tune? Nor do you.

Do you remember our breakfast?
We started with 'Let us all pray';
The oysters we ate from the river
were living. (And so, nor do they.)

The Picnic Kit

Do you remember our picnics?
Sandwiches, boiled eggs and cheese,
lemonade spilling from beakers,
hayfever sneezes and bees.

Everyone packed up the hamper
and though it may now seem absurd
spaces were left in the basket
to fit in a very small bird.

Ever delighted by music
we took such a creature along,
eating the left over biscuits,
giving amusement with song.

When we were all feeling tired
reaching the end of the day
then we would repack the hamper
letting the bird fly away.

Last christmas we all got together
and we ate the last goose that we'd saved.
'Twas the last time we saw Auntie Heather
'cos Auntie Maud's cat misbehaved.

Last christmas Papa bought a reindeer,
to pull our toboggan, he said.
But it rained for the whole of december
so it played the piano instead.

when we visited Auntie last Christmas
we all found it awfully weird:
there were sixpences found in the
birdcage
and the budgie had quite disappeared.

If you want Christmas delivered half price
or presents presented or refuse removal
come to our company, we'll do the job;
(just take the word of a seal of approval).

PENGUIN DE MILO

You cannot say
this bird is tuneful
but rather it's
a healthy spoonful.

A PARROT ON A PERCH

can a bird untie a knot? can it find Lord Lucan?
can it carry heavy weights? (one cannot but two can).

A cherry's a berry to eat on its own.
In the soft centre you'll find there's a stone,
once it's removed you must eat the flesh whole
for these are the fruits of which life is a bowl.

PIGS

a pig in a poke – a blind purchase: a poke
   is a bag. often there was a cat
   inside the bag to swindle the
   naive purchaser, who, on
   returning home, would "let the
   cat out of the bag." (a poke
   can also be a bonnet.)

to teach a pig to play the flute – to
   attempt the impossible.

pig months – september to april (those
   with an 'r' in them).

go at it like a pig at a tater – to act like
   a bull in a china shop.

the pig's eye – the ace of diamonds.

to drive one's pigs to market – to snore.

memories of childhood often
evoke
a poke in the eye or a pig in
a poke.

Come inside and wash your hands
and take your finger out of there.
Where's the clothes brush? Do you know?
Go; run along and comb your hair.

Sit up to the breakfast bar,
eat your porridge nicely, dear.
Don't eat honey from the jar:
your manners don't improve, I fear.

Soon we'll all have jam for tea
and then we can indulge ourselves
on lobsters taken from the sea
and owls from supermarket shelves.

READ THIS IN THE MIRROR
BY THE LIGHT OF ANY MOON
SO THE FUTURE LIES BEHIND YOU
AND THE PAST WILL BE HERE SOON

46

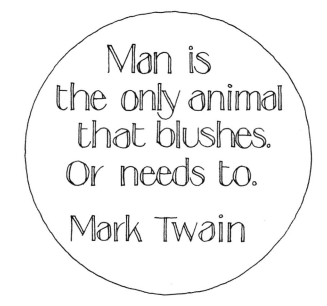

Man is
the only animal
that blushes.
Or needs to.

Mark Twain

simon drew